PENTECOST

By

DONALD GEE

Gospel Publishing House

Springfield, Mo., U. S. A.

2-569

CONTENTS

(Printed in United States of America)

1

MY PERSONAL TESTIMONY TO PENTECOST

BY THE grace of God I definitely and personally accepted the Lord Jesus Christ as my Saviour in October, 1905, when Seth Joshua, one of the preachers of the Welsh Revival, conducted a special mission in the Congregational Church in North London, of which my mother was a member. My father had died when I was nine years' old.

Soon afterwards I became a member of the church also, and for seven years I threw myself into all its activities heart and soul, until there was scarcely an organization of the church with which I was not connected in some way or another. On the whole, however, I leaned more and more towards the purely social and worldly side of church life, although at the same time there was another side of me which was craving for spiritual satisfaction, and would take an interest in anything that seemed to possess spiritual reality. Things came to a crisis at a Communion service when I was horribly startled to find that when I was in the very act of taking the bread and the wine I was nevertheless thinking all the while of flippant talk I had engaged in the day before in the tennis club with another of the church members sitting just in front of me. This set me seriously considering my spiritual condition.

About the same time, my mother was very earnestly seeking a fuller life in Christ, and was baptized by immersion in a near-by Baptist Church. I attended the service, but was in a furious temper, and was ready to knock a friendly deacon down who suggested that I might take the same step at the next service. Nevertheless God was speaking to me, and in February, 1912, I was baptized myself in another Baptist Church, though still retaining my membership as a Congregationalist. My fiancee, now my wife, was baptized at the same service. Satan resisted this step with all his power, and just before I went out to the service that night I felt as if my very reason would snap as a result of the intensity of the spiritual conflict. It was the same when I came home, after having been baptized, and it was not till about 3:30 the next morning that I came into peace by definitely standing in faith upon Rom. 6:4. Then the Lord spoke into my heart the promise "Thou shalt not pass this way again." It has been blessedly true that I have never since experienced the same awful spiritual conflict that I went through over baptism in water.

Just then my mother had been introduced to a missionary, home on furlough from India, who had received the Baptism in the Holy Spirit, and had spoken in tongues as in the New Testament (Acts 2:4), at Pandita Ramabai's, Mukti, during the wonderful revival which God had given there. This sister had gone out to India from a Baptist Church, and we had heard rumors of some strange experience she had passed through out in India, which some attributed to sunstroke! We felt a little nervous when first introduced to her as we were warned she might be a little strange. We soon found that she was perfectly sane and normal however, and as a matter of fact she was rejoicing in just that satisfying Christian experience that we were longing for. Nevertheless I was still fighting the truth, and when this friend paid visits to us to talk to my mother, I would sit down at the piano and thump out oratorio music as loudly as I could, to try and make conversation difficult. The missionary took it all very sweetly, and that impressed me the more.

In the summer of 1912 I went to my first Pentecostal meeting. I was really hungry for God, and while on holiday in the Isle of Wight was invited by a local preacher in the Methodist Church to attend a small meeting held in a railway mission at the back of Ryde. Mr. E. W. Moser, of Southsea, crossed over every Monday to conduct this meeting. The conduct of the meeting seemed very strange to me, after the formal prayer meetings I was used to; but I was very much impressed when for the first time I actually heard in that meeting for myself the "speaking with tongues" of which I had now heard so much. I had no question of this being a perfectly Scriptural manifestation.

Before returning to India, our missionary friend had introduced my mother to Pentecostal meetings in London, and she was going regularly. But I would have nothing of them, and truth to tell felt rather scared of both Pentecostal people and their meetings.

Then there came one never-to-be-forgotten night in January, 1913, when a whole night of prayer was to be held at the Missionary Rest Home of Mrs. Cantel, 73 Highbury New Park, London. My mother wished to go, but to return home at midnight. I did not like to let her come through the streets of London alone at that hour (although she was perfectly willing), and so, with very bad grace, I agreed to accompany her, simply to act as an escort. But at that memorable meeting God gripped me. I can see the wisdom of God now in that the first hymn was of a type more familiar to me; "O God our help in ages past"; and this made me feel at home. I had never heard such praying; they prayed as though God was intensely real, and as though His Presence was actually in the room, which indeed was true. When we left at midnight, I was asking the date of the next meeting! From that night I was suddenly and completely weaned from all the old relationships in the church I had been attending since a child. Although still fulfilling certain duties as assistant organist, I was at every possible meeting at "No. 73," and cannot speak too highly of the kind sympathy and help extended by dear Sister Cantel, now with the Lord.

Though now fully convinced of the truth of the Pentecostal testimony, and thoroughly enjoying the meetings, I made no immediate attempt to seek the Baptism of the Holy Spirit for myself. I think I was partly put off by the reports I continually heard of seekers who were having to "wait" a long while, and I thought it must inevitably be a dry, weary business. So I postponed it, but enjoyed the meetings.

However, one Wednesday night in March, 1913, I played for the mid-week service at the Congregational Church (which finished promptly at 9 p. m.), and then ran all the way to enjoy the remainder of the meeting in Highbury New Park. After it had concluded (about 10:30 p. m.), the brother who had been conducting it, a respected minister from Ireland, put me through a sort of catechism. "Was I saved?"—Yes. "Was I baptized?"—Yes. "Was I baptized in the Holy Spirit?"—No. "Then why not?" I explained my aversion to the apparently weary "waiting" times. He electrified me by telling me they were not an essential. Opening his Bible he read to me Luke 11:13, and then Mark 11:24, and then asked me if I believed these verses. I assured him that I did, and as I declared my faith it seemed as if God dropped down into my heart from heaven an absolute assurance that these promises were now being actually fulfilled in me. I had no immediate manifestation, but went home supremely happy, having received the Baptism of the Holy Spirit "by faith." I clearly realized, however, that the experience I had believed God's Word for involved a Scriptural manifestation of the Spirit as in the book of Acts and so I fully expected this, and had no thought of anything else.

From that hour my joy and gladness was intense, until I hardly knew how to express myself when in prayer and praise. The assurance that God had indeed fulfilled His promise to me gathered in certainty. I experienced a new fullness beyond words, and found it becoming increasingly difficult to adequately voice all the glory in my soul. This went on for about two weeks, and then one night, when praying all alone by my bedside before retiring, and when once again finding no English adequate to express the overflowing fullness of my soul, I found myself beginning to utter words in a new tongue. I was in a condition of spiritual ecstasy, and taken up wholly with the Lord. For the first time I personally tasted the experience referred to in 1 Cor. 14:2.

Increasing glory now flooded my soul in the meetings as well, until I began to speak in new tongues publicly. Also I would sing very much in the Spirit in new tongues, when the little Assembly would be moved in this way by the Holy Spirit during our times of prayer and worship. My whole Christian experience was revolutionized. I was no longer seeking here and there for spiritual satisfaction—I had found. All my delight was in prayer, and Bible study, and Christian fellowship. This was only about six weeks before my marriage, and an old Baptist minister, who came to try and argue me out of my new-found blessing, was compelled to admit that he had never known a young man so near such a happy event and yet so filled with interest in spiritual things. My wife, happily, was wholly one with me; and we were rejoicing together.

Immediately I threw myself heart and soul into Pentecostal meetings, and benefited inestimably by the faithful ministry of the Word I there received. During the World War I felt a clear call of God in my heart to the work of ministry, and began to preach in small meetings here and there, as doors opened. Finally, in 1920, I accepted an invitation to Edinburgh to take charge of Pentecostal work there, and gave up my business in London altogether. Since then, by the blessing of God, this has grown into a splendidly established church, full of evangelical and missionary zeal, and with many activities among young and old. A ministry by pen has developed until it is touching every corner of the globe; and writings on various Scriptural subjects, and especially concerning Spiritual Gifts, have been translated into many different languages, and appear in many different religious periodicals over all the world. The Lord has graciously given an ever increasing ministry of His precious word of truth, until the last few years it has become literally world-wide. Bible Study Campaigns have been held in the principal cities of Australia, New Zealand, the U. S., Canada, as well as over all the British Isles. This is being written in Finland, where night after night large halls are crowded out, with many standing for over two hours to hear the Word of God expounded. Souls are being saved, and believers of many different denominations blessed and revived. The Holy Spirit is being poured out upon hungry souls. To God alone be all the glory! These things are attributable to nothing but the gifts of the Spirit which He has graciously placed within the "earthen vessel" (Rom. 12:3; 2 Cor. 4:7).

When asked to sum up the results of "Pentecost" in my own personal experience, I always delight to give one answer: "It has made the Lord Jesus intensely *real*."

2

"HE SHALL BAPTIZE YOU WITH THE HOLY GHOST"

A Letter to an Enquirer

Dear Friend:

You interest me very much when you tell me that you recently heard the testimony of S. J., and that he is now claiming to have received "the Baptism in the Holy Ghost."

You say that there can be no doubt that he is vastly changed as a Christian from when you last met him two years ago; nowadays he is so full of love, so full of zeal and enthusiasm for God and for souls, for times of prayer and Christian fellowship, for the Bible—that he truly seems "turned into another man."

I am not in the least surprised that you admit that all this is making you hungry for a similar blessing for yourself; nor am I unduly surprised at the hesitation which at the same time you feel regarding committing yourself to a path that seems so unlike all we have become accustomed to in our own church and Christian experience. I can quite enter into those mixed feelings of yours when you accompanied him for the first time the other night to a "Pentecostal" meeting.

You felt greatly drawn to the life and liberty of the place, the hearty singing, the fervent prayers, and particularly—I am pleased to note—the preaching of the Word; all combining to make the Bible seem a beautifully up-to-date Book after all. Nevertheless you found the "noise" rather trying, especially during prayer; it was so unlike what we are used to. Moreover, you could not quite understand when a sister spoke in "tongues," though you say you certainly found the "interpretation" given by the pastor most helpful, and coming like a real message straight from God to your own soul.

You ask me for some Scriptural basis for all this, and I appreciate the candor with which you express yourself, provided it stands the test of God's Book—as ready to follow all clearer light which God may have for you in these things, even at the cost of breaking with preconceived ideas and, if necessary, old associations.

I believe that we can get almost all the light we need just at the moment from the third chapter of Luke, or the parallel chapter in Matthew 3.

In order to be sure, first of all, that in speaking of "the baptism with the Holy Ghost" we are using a Scriptural term, and describing a proper Scriptural experience, turn to verse 16.

You will find here a prophecy by John of the future ministry of Jesus which is equally recorded by each of the other Evangelists. Matt. 3:11; Mark 1:8; John 1:33. I need not remind you that our blessed Lord never fulfilled this prophecy in His earthly ministry; and it will come rushing to your mind at once that the first great fulfillment was on the Day of Pentecost, after His ascension to the Father's right hand. Acts 2:33. From then on we find Him continually exercising this glorious prerogative (Acts 4:31; 8:17; 9:17; 10:44; 19:6), and Peter links the experience of those Gentiles in the house of Cornelius, for instance, with this prophecy given years before by John, beyond all contradiction or uncertainty. Acts 11: 16, 17.

We all believe that until our Lord's return He will still remain in that blessed place of power on high. Is there one single passage in the Bible to make us think that He would cease to bestow this Divine Gift in like manner ? The biggest argument against such an experience for today comes—not from inside the Bible, but outside—from the lack of Pentecostal manifestation in most of His professing church. But is such an argument valid? Is this God's responsibility—or man's? We all know that whenever the Church has roused herself to make fresh claims for Pentecostal power and fullness, her Lord has never failed to answer by revival upon revival. The grand charter of her birthright in Acts 2:39 still holds good.

You particularly ask me as to what we ought to expect when we receive the Baptism of the Spirit: and evidently your question frames itself principally around certain outward manifestations which you have either seen or heard of in those receiving this blessing.

Turning again to the third chaper of Luke, shall we place ourselves among the crowd that first heard this expression "baptize you with the Holy Ghost and fire" come from the lips of John, and try to gather the impression such words would give them of the sort of experience that was intended. The Baptist was not the sort of preacher to leave folk in much uncertainty as to what he meant.

He was telling them of an experience necessarily mysterious, and, as yet, entirely in the future for them all: but he linked it by one forceful word with something now familiar and constantly being enacted before their eyes—*"baptize."*

There was to be something about this experience, then, that would be like baptism in water—only far mightier. That John baptized by immersion is not a point many will care to dispute, and therefore the first conception these people would gain would be of a complete immersion in the Spirit of God. This, in itself, would indicate something overwhelming to the entire being.

Baptism by immersion was, and is, such an

absolutely *real* experience: so conscious to the candidate, so evident to the onlooker. Evidently this greater Baptism will also be an absolutely *real* experience also; something that the recipient will feel supremely conscious of, something equally evident to the one standing by.

Lest I seem straining our parallel (it is far more than a "type," for both experiences should still continue hand in hand), remember that both these features—conscious experience to the recipient and manifestation to the onlooker—are found in the New Testament instances.

Conscious experience of the Baptism with the Holy Spirit was so overwhelming on the Day of Pentecost that they even appeared to be "drunk with new wine" to the crowd that gathered. Acts 2:13. Evidence, even more convincing to others perhaps than to the recipients themselves that some mighty new power had possessed them, was provided both at Pentecost and after by utterance in "tongues" and prophecy. Acts 2:4, 17; 10:46; 19:6. Simon must have seen something very real take place at Samaria (Acts 8:18), even though he himself was unhappily without the blessing.

Receiving the Baptism in the Holy Ghost in New Testament times was a real and vivid experience as we can well imagine. In this it is quite distinct from the New Birth, which often takes place unconsciously at the moment (John 3:8), or at least without outward manifestation. But the moment of one's Baptism in the Spirit may well be the supreme moment of spiritual, and even physical, consciousness in the whole life.

Why should it be otherwise? Is it not quite strangely illogical as well as un-Scriptural to expect anything else? Consider what actually takes place. I have spoken of an "experience," a "blessing," a "gift": but the truth is bigger than all these terms. It is *God Himself* coming to fill the "earthen vessel": it is the infinite enfolding the finite. No wonder the child of God is not only spiritually, but usually physically, overwhelmed when this happens. Blessed overwhelming!

I have somewhat stressed this point because I not only want to ease any fears by showing you how perfectly Scriptural, normal, and logical, physical manifestations are when receiving the Baptism in the Holy Spirit: but I would also fain deliver you from ever settling down to satisfaction with an experience short of the Scripture, by showing you the actual incompleteness, as measured by God's standards, of experiences received "by faith" *without any* outward manifestation. The Book that tells of those who received the Spirit "by faith," also describes the character of the experience they then received.

You may probably stumble at first over the teaching that the Scriptural evidence of the Baptism in the Holy Spirit is speaking with other tongues; and that it should always be expected in every case as an initial "sign"; though not always a permanent "gift." 1 Cor. 12:30. Yet I firmly believe that if you ponder this with an open heart and mind before the Lord, you will come to see from the examples and significance of the recorded cases in the New Testament (Acts 2:4; 8:18; 10:44-47; 19:6) that it is really so; and that after all this strange sign unquestionably marks the divine choice for a simple, universal and supernatural evidence to seal the Baptism with the Spirit. Men did not choose it in the first century, neither do they choose it in the twentieth. "What was I that I could withstand God?" was Peter's defense on this very point: the apology today for what seems so offensive to many is based on identically the same ground.

I must close now; I am sure there will be other phases of this entrancing subject which we shall want to go into later on. Meanwhile—you are hungry? I know that your candor in voicing these questions and difficulties springs not from opposition to anything you sincerely believe may be of God—but only from a desire to remove obstacles.

My closing counsel can again find foothold in the scenes of Luke 3. As one after another sought baptism in water in those days from the Baptist, you know what it involved—preparation and yielding. It is so with this greater Baptism. You are already a believer. I urge you in a fuller way than ever before to lay hold upon the perfect cleansing from all sin provided for us in the blood of Jesus. If the Lord shows you anything to be given up, anything to be put right, any matter of obedience to His will —obey Him instantly. Do not be in any way artificial in these things, however; only obey rigidly the voice of God.

And when you ask the Lord Jesus to baptize you with the Holy Ghost, beloved, do yield to Him. *Let* Him do it. It was necessary for that crowd to trust the Baptist implicitly as he laid each one beneath the waters of Jordan. When your own beloved pastor immersed you in like fashion not long since, you willingly surrendered yourself wholly into his hands; he could not possibly have baptized you otherwise, however much both he and you desired it. Will you trust Jesus less?

If anyone had suggested to you that your pastor would permit some evil to befall you when you asked for baptism—how scornfully you would have repudiated the idea! And rightly so. Will your Saviour prove any less faithful?

Ask Him. Talk it over with the Lord Jesus. Do not seek manifestation, or gift, or experience—just seek Him. And you will find that He will meet you in the good old Bible way and make your life fragrant with

His presence and your testimony convincing with His power.

Before we next meet I expect to hear that you are rejoicing in personal enjoyment of what I have tried to write a little about. I believe God has marked your readiness to receive His promise, and I am persuaded that He has thus brought this pregnant question right into your life at this time, not merely for your interest, but for you to "go in and possess." May He help you.

With every good wish,

Yours sincerely,

DONALD GEE

3

TO SEEKERS AFTER THE BAPTISM IN THE HOLY GHOST

Three questions will probably be asked by sincerely interested and seeking souls concerning the glorious experience that we who have received usually call the Baptism in the Holy Ghost: (1) What is this experience? (2) How can I receive this blessing? (3) How can I *know* I have received?

What Is the Baptism in the Holy Ghost?

To most of us, this has been a perfectly distinct experience from our conversion, and to this agrees the clear testimony of the Scriptures—Acts 8:16; 9:17; 19:2, etc. The instance of Cornelius (Acts 10:44) remains as a blessed proof that it is possible for God to sweep a new convert instantly into the fullness of the Spirit; but in actual fact this is the experience of very few.

When you are baptized in the Holy Ghost you *know* it, and need no one to acquaint you with the fact; bless God, you will soon be acquainting them. When you are baptized in the Holy Ghost, *God touches you* and for ever after in your life you know God touched you, and that He lives. In the final analysis, the Baptism in the Spirit is not a doctrine but an experience, and the test of whether I have received is not a cleverly woven doctrine that will include me within its borders, but whether I know the experience in burning *fact* in heart and life.

What is this blessing? It is impossible to define that which God intends to be limitless in words or terms, but we suggest that there are two sides—God's and mine. God's side is that when a believer is filled with His Spirit He at last comes in to possess the *whole*. It takes a little while before we begin to appreciate God's side of "Pentecost." At first we are very naturally taken up with our own side, with the overflowing joy, with the glory in our souls, the manifestations, the new experiences; and no wonder! But later on we begin to enter into His joy, and it is often too deep for words as at last we see the Lord "possessing His possessions," and getting hold of a life to henceforth hold it and send it forth with every power developed, and kept tuned to highest pitch, in His service among men. If *we* have joy when we see the Lord baptizing in the Holy Ghost, we may be sure that He has a greater.

An experience that has been the uncomfortable lot of a good many in England in recent years seems to give a very adequate illustration here. During the shortage of houses, a desirable dwelling offered for sale has been purchased on the understanding that the existing tenants would very soon move out and give the owner occupation; but how often, for various reasons, the promised occupation has not been forthcoming, and disappointment has filled many waiting months. But at last the house is vacated, and the rightful owner receives the occupation he has been longing for and has paid for. How true a picture this is of God's side of the Baptism. The "house" (Paul calls it a "temple") has been already purchased by nothing less than the precious blood of Christ; but in how many cases the Lord is still longing and waiting for complete possession, even if we have given Him one or two rooms as it were. The old tenants of self and self-will have lingered and have been unwilling to surrender all.

When God baptizes you in the Holy Ghost, every key is given up, every door thrown open wide, and at last the Lord of Glory possesses entirely that which He died to make His own. Hallelujah! No wonder the shouts of glory make the places ring where *this* is taking place; it is something to shout about. God comes into His own, and His purpose henceforth is nothing less than a life filled with His presence, fragrant with His beauty, mighty with His power.

And what about our side of the experience? For us it marks the entrance into an entirely new sphere, a lifting by Almighty grace to "higher ground," the opening of a new chapter, we almost said a new volume, of Christian experience.

If it is true that God comes into our poor lives, it is also true that we become lost in God. A new sense, a spiritual sense, seems added, and we become alive to that which before was meaningless. A little one in the home who is just learning to read, and thereby entering into an entirely new world of interest and possibility, seems to provide us at the moment with just the illustration that we need. A new realm opens up to our view. As the Holy Spirit takes full control, we rejoice in God as one who has made a new discovery; indeed, *a personal "Pentecost" IS a new discovery of the Living Christ.*

We are taken into God, and the soul will receive a consuming desire to ever more be utterly and entirely lost in Him. A drinking vessel plunged beneath the waters, and then lifted up, sparkling and overflowing, that thirsty souls may drink, can typify the life of the Spirit-filled ministry the Lord intends toward others; but it is when the vessel is again taken and plunged beneath the waters, entirely hidden but filled with the fullness all around it, that the soul's deepest inner life and inner desire is typified, glory be to God!

"Pentecost" *does* bring us into a new sphere of things spiritually; we desire to affirm this very humbly but very decidedly; humbly, because it is all of God's grace and there is no room for pride, but firmly because definite and supernatural experiences are God's determined answer to the devil's counterfeits, and the world's "higher critical" unbelief and materialism of the hour.

How Can I Receive This Blessing?

Any teaching here is intended to help, not to make cast iron roads on which we practically demand God to work. Thank God, we have proved that He meets individual cases in an infinite variety of ways, and the Almighty will not be bound to our limited conception of His ways of working. Nevertheless the Scriptures are our infallible guide to a better understanding of His ways, and to believers hungry for the Baptism of the Holy Ghost we would always say first of all —fulfill the conditions of Acts 2:38.

"Repent":—the essential element in true repentance is reality, a willingness, a determination to do business with God, to put the life right, to prove sincerity in seeking God by actual fruit in a changed life. "And be baptized":—without detracting one jot from the force of a literal application of this to believer's immersion—we heartily believe in it,—we also want to see behind it the whole principle of obedience, obedience to everything and anything that God may require. The Lord may often prove our willingness to obey by testing on just one little point—a mere detail of life in itself, but revealing infallibly the purpose of the heart within. We remember a brother who was seeking the Baptism, and every time he got to prayer the

Lord brought before him a caged linnet that was hanging up in the kitchen window. Someone had captured the little wild bird and made him a present of it, but God tested the whole principle of this brother's obedience by whether he would let it go free. It was a struggle—and let those who smile search their own hearts,—but at last one Saturday afternoon when he came home from the shop the bird was set free, and in a short time so was its late master, and gloriously filled with the Spirit of God. Have you any "linnets" that God is talking to *you* about?

The next requirement that we would put before those seeking the Baptism is faith in the promises on this subject. Turn for example to Acts 2:39 and Luke 11:13 (there are others also). Do you whole-heartedly believe these promises, and stand on them with a definite personal acceptance that they are for you? Do not come to God for the Baptism merely because someone else has had a big blessing, and you would like to be as happy and overflowing as they are. We strongly urge you to search the Scripture and make sure of your personal claim to this inheritance of all true believers. It is only if you are "standing on the promises," both before and after being baptized in the Spirit, that you will prevail "when the howling storms of doubt and fear assail."

One more word to those seeking this blessing: repent, obey, believe—and then "tarry until." A real, Scriptural Baptism in the Spirit means a definite act of the risen and glorified Lord Jesus. We cannot baptize ourselves, neither can we do more than lead one another to the place of blessing; it is *His* glorious work to immerse in the Holy Ghost. My taking "by faith" is right and proper—believing the promises is always God's turnpike road to blessing; but let us repeat, the Baptism of the Holy Ghost is a real, definite, vivid experience, and do not be satisfied until you *are* satisfied.

While tarrying for the Promise of the Father, maintain an attitude of continual, expectant faith,—always believe that God is going to meet you *now*. We would recommend praising the Lord, but always with sincerity; *never* merely repeating any formula of praise mechanically. But praise brings victory, it stimulates faith, it makes the devil run, and brings the soul into the very presence of God. Do not bury your face in your hands or in some cushion in the depths of an easy chair; let your face catch the attitude of your soul and be thrown upward to the glory, and then "let go and let God." Let every door of your whole being be open wide, your whole soul occupied with Jesus, and verily, the King of glory shall soon find an abundant entrance.

Our last question must be dealt with very faithfully—

How Shall I Know I have Received?

Quite a common and popular, and certainly very precious teaching is that we know He has come because as the weeks and months go by, we find a new power stealing into our lives, and new beauty becoming manifest in our character before others. Yet this is substituting "fruit" of the Spirit for the "manifestation" of the Spirit, two quite distinct operations of God. The fruit of the Spirit (and God grant it in all our lives) is the proof of our walking in the Spirit (Gal. 5:16, 22, 25), not the proof of our being baptized in the Spirit. Fruit always takes time to grow; many months, sometimes years, elapse between the planting of the orchard and the bearing of the precious fruit. But the divinely appointed proof of the coming of the Comforter is something given instantly, on the spot, at the time.

We never read in the New Testament that they put Cornelius or others on probation for a time to see by their lives whether they had received the Holy Ghost; His coming was something God bore witness to instantly and convincingly. Let us not hesitate to boldly declare that God's divinely chosen sign of the coming of the Holy Ghost to fill His temple is a supernatural manifestation given at the moment; no other doctrine fulfills the demands of Scripture, no other doctrine so thoroughly fulfills the demands of reason;

we are on unshakable ground here, and need fear the attacks of none.

Only one word remains;—what are the New Testament manifestations given with this experience? Several may be named; "wind," "fire," "tongues," "prophecy," etc.; the final choice of the Holy Spirit both then and now seems to rest on speaking in a new tongue.

Why cavil at God's choice? Much could be written from personal experience of the use and blessing of this manifestation; particularly when receiving the Baptism; but God has chosen it for His sign, and the rather we would simply accept it—humbly, cheerfully, adoringly.

And then go forth, filled with His power, to a life of faithful service and testimony among men, till our Lord shall come and "gather the reapers Home."

4

KEEPING FILLED WITH THE SPIRIT

"Be filled with the Spirit." Eph. 5:18.

We sometimes hear the above scripture quoted as an exhortation to seek the Baptism in the Spirit, but that is taking it out of its setting. These people had received the fullness of the Spirit. In Acts 19 we read that when the Apostle Paul laid his hands on them the Holy Ghost came upon them and they spoke with tongues and prophesied. Now he writes, "You Pentecostal people, be filled with the Spirit."

First of all I want to say that a condition of being filled with the Spirit is *recognizable;* you cannot be filled with the Spirit and not know it, and you cannot be filled with the Spirit and other people not know it. The apostles told them to look out seven men of honest report (and that came first), and full of the Holy Ghost; but how could they have picked out seven men full of the Holy Ghost if they had not known who was filled. It must be a recognizable condition. There are signs which indicate the condition of keeping filled with the Spirit.

As verse 18 tells us to be filled with the Spirit, so do verses 19, 20 and 21 tell us the marks of those who are thus filled. "Speaking to yourselves in psalms and hymns and spiritual songs, singing and making melody in your heart to the Lord." I believe the first mark of being filled with the Spirit is an overflowing testimony. The cup is full and running over. The verse does not say you have to be making a noise all the time; it says "making melody *in your heart.*" My precious brother, if you have not got that song in your heart perhaps you are not filled with the Spirit, perhaps you have leaked out somewhere. You answer, "I received the Baptism two years ago." Yes, my brother, but where are you now? Oh the people who talk about past experiences! If you have a fresh experience you have a song inside.

Never will I forget when Dr. Slocum of India came to Edinburgh and I went to the station to meet him. When he got off the train we shook hands and strolled down to the entrance of the station to get the street car. He stopped at the sidewalk and looked me in the face and said, "Brother Gee, you are under the burden, you are carrying the strain." He had diagnosed me in three minutes and fifty seconds and knew very well I was not where I ought to be. Spiritual health is as evident as natural health; the fullness of the Holy Ghost is as apparent as the fullness of the life which God has given in the body. Paul says that if you are filled with the Spirit you will be singing to yourselves psalms and hymns and spiritual songs.

And though troubles may surge around, there will even be songs in the night. They may be in the minor key, but the finest music is in the minor. Nothing can stop the man from singing who is filled with the Spirit. That is the first mark.

The next verse gives us another mark—"Giving thanks always for all things unto God and the Father in the name of our Lord Jesus Christ." You say, "I was neglected in the assembly; they did not give me the position I wanted." Well, give thanks for it, then you will know you are filled with the Spirit. God has taught me one golden secret—that the key to victory in every situation is to get down and thank Him for what has happened. The first lesson I learned on this line was a very sharp one. Somebody came to our city and started an opposition assembly. They opened a meeting quite near at hand, and personally visited all my members, even making nasty remarks about me. My temptation was to get bitter, to fight, to stand on the platform and (so to speak) take my jacket off and roll up my sleeves. But how I do thank God that just in the nick of time He showed me the victory. And I have found that if you become bitter and fight, your people will get hardened and the Holy Ghost will be grieved and driven away.

So instead of fighting I said, "Thank You, Lord." Evidently I was not praying enough and I needed something to make me pray more. Or perhaps my preaching was not good enough. I have discovered that competition is good even in the kingdom of God. While in business I found that competition was the life of trade, but when I came into the ministry I said, "I have said good-bye to competition." But I hadn't. Competition is the best thing for some preachers; it pulls them up. God can sanctify all these things. Do not misunderstand me; I do not infer that the man who started a competition assembly was showing a right spirit. But I do mean that there is a place of victory in every situation, and that place of victory is "giving thanks always for all things." When the trial comes, say, "Praise the Lord, I guess it is good for me, I guess I needed it, it will be good for me later on, afterward it will yield the peaceable fruit of righteousness." If you do that, people will know you are filled with the Spirit. But if you go around grumbling and whining they will doubt whether you are filled with the Spirit at all.

The third mark is the greatest of all. First, an overflowing testimony; second, giving thanks always for all things. But listen to the third, "Submitting yourselves one to another in the fear of God." I believe the finest evidence of being filled with the Spirit is a brokenness and humility. Are they not choice! They make it easy to submit to the other fellow. In my ministry of teaching I find such a difference in people. When you bring some people the Word of God they get offended. Others say, "Pooh! I don't agree with you." And some people cannot be taught anything. But when people are really filled with the Holy Ghost they are teachable. You may speak in tongues a great deal, but if you have not a teachable spirit I question what manner of spirit you are of.

Teachers are not perfect and their teaching is sometimes imperfect; sometimes you may have a right to question what they say and to disagree with them. But if you have the Spirit of God in you, you will question them meekly, you will keep brotherly; and instead of getting offended and going away in a huff you will go to the teacher in a sweet and gracious spirit and will say, "Perhaps I did not quite understand you or catch your meaning." Oh how lovely is this spirit of submitting ourselves one to another in the fear of God.

Some time ago I was holding a series of meetings. When we got down to pray at the close of a meeting, there was a woman who had a voice like a siren and who seemed to think the proper thing to do when you prayed was to make a noise like a train going through a railroad tunnel. When she made this terrific noise I felt it was often unnecessary, that it was not of the Spirit but that it was her own feelings expressing themselves in that way. It was so disturbing, for no one could pray; it was distracting; she filled the program with her noise, and the noise could be heard two or three blocks away. One of the gifts God has given is the gift of government, and we have to govern —not in the flesh, but in the Spirit. And so I gave a little teaching on those things. We never heard any more of the screeching. The last evening I was there she came and grasped my hand, saying with tears in her eyes, "O Brother Gee, I do thank God for the teaching you have given me. You know I did not want to do anything wrong, or to disturb the people, but I thought I had to do that to yield to the Holy Ghost. But since you have opened the Word I see differently now." A teachable spirit is a lovely thing. God give it to every one of us, and most of all to the teachers themselves. Directly I find myself getting resentful when men don't agree with me, or getting angry if they dare to criticize what I write or speak, I say, "Donald Gee, be careful, the thermometer is going down."

But the most practical and important part of our study is coming now—how to *keep* filled with the Spirit. Eighteen years have rolled by since the Lord baptized me in the Holy Spirit, and today I have a passion as never before to be filled with the Spirit. How can we keep filled with the Spirit as the years roll by?

I could bring you a good many theories and thoughts of my own but I prefer to stick to the Book. "Then Peter, filled with the

Holy Ghost, said unto them." Acts 4:8. Peter had had the Baptism in the Spirit but now he gets another filling. Some time had elapsed since Pentecost, but he is still filled, In Acts 4:31 it says, "And when they had prayed, the place was shaken where they were assembled together; and they were all filled with the Holy Ghost, and they spake the word of God with boldness." Look again at Acts 7:55, "But Stephen, being full of the Holy Ghost, looked up stedfastly into heaven." And Acts 13:52. "And the disciples were filled with joy and with the Holy Ghost." Examine these four passages carefully and you will find the first condition for keeping filled with the Spirit is bold testimony. Here is Peter standing before the council. They order him not to preach any more in the name of Jesus. But Peter is as bold and brave as a lion; he tells them we ought to obey God rather than men; and the consequence is he gets filled with the Spirit.

In the next case the church is being threatened and they get down to pray. Is this how they pray, "O Lord, behold their threatenings and hide us away in some corner where they won't find us. Take care of us, please don't let them touch us." Is that how they prayed? Oh, the magnificent tone of their prayer as they said, "Now Lord, behold their threatenings; and grant unto thy servants that with all boldness they may speak thy word, by stretching forth thine hand to heal;

and that signs and wonders may be done by the name of thy holy child Jesus." If there is one thing that stirs the enemy up it is signs and wonders. They prayed a brave prayer, they did not go on the policy of Safety First. God save us from that policy in the church. Instead of saying Safety First, they said, "Lord, send the power!" Stephen is brought before the council and he boldly testifies. The consequence is he is filled with the Spirit and his face is as the face of an angel.

Now what about ourselves? Many a Pentecostal preacher has lost the anointing through compromise, and so has many a Pentecostal believer. If you want to keep filled with the Spirit, the Lord help you to have a bold, uncompromising, unquenchable testimony wherever you go. I think of some men who were leaders of the Pentecostal movement in Great Britain in the beginning; mighty men, filled with the Holy Ghost. But they tried to put the new wine of the Pentecostal experience into the old bottles of formalism. And if you try experiments like that I want to give you a straight word from the Lord Jesus. He said that you cannot put the new wine in old bottles, and if you do there is an explosion, the bottle cracks and you lose the wine. Those men dried up.

I believe that bold witnessing is one of the reasons for persecution, and persecution is one of the things that keeps the fire burning. I am a little concerned when I find people getting too respectable. They may have fine churches with lovely carpet on the floor, they may have pipe organs and choirs; but I hope the Lord will put the poker in soon and stir them up. I say this solemnly. The supernatural is beginning to wane in some places. I go to some assemblies where they never have a message in tongues or interpretation, where they have never heard the gift of prophecy, where the meeting is carried on like machinery and clockwork, and you always know what is going to happen next in the program. A Pentecostal meeting where you always know what is going to happen next is backslidden.

There is another case in Acts 13:9 of being filled with the Spirit after receiving the Baptism. Paul had been filled with the Holy Ghost long ago, and God had blessed his ministry. But that day he was standing on the threshold of something new; and as he faced the old sorcerer he was filled with the Spirit, and there was power that he had not known before. In this case the keynote was obedience. Paul and Barnabas had been in Antioch, and oh, what a nice little nest they had there, and they were so happy and comfortable. They were right in the middle of having a few days of prayer and conviction and waiting on God when the Holy Ghost said, "Separate me Paul and Barnabas." "Oh, but Lord, we don't want to go, we are so comfortable here and have such a lovely church." "Come along, I can look after that." "Oh, but Lord, we are buying a car on the installment plan. Lord, we would have to leave our families and live in two suitcases." "Come along." Thank God, they obeyed; and as Paul stepped out in a new pathway of obedience God met him with a new fullness of the Holy Ghost.

If there is anything in your heart that you know God has called you to obey Him over, and you are not obeying, you will lose the anointing. But if you will obey you will keep the anointing. I would rather lose everything than lose the anointing. That is more important than anything. I have had to swallow my own sermon. I had a lovely assembly and I said I would never leave it, I was going to be a "life-pastor." A broody hen with her chickens under her wings, saying Cluck, Cluck, all the time! And when the Lord told me to leave it and to live in two suitcases, oh how I struggled. Then the Lord showed me something that filled me with terror. He seemed to say, "If you want to keep that assembly, all right, but you will dry up on the spot." I had to choose between drying up in Edinburgh or traveling around from place to place. I was able to say, "Yes," and only God knows the joy He has given me as I have been conscious of the gracious anointing of the Spirit upon His word.

Continued fullness marked the character of

Barnabas. "For he was a good man and full of the Holy Ghost and faith." Acts 11:24. What was the keynote of the fullness that was marking him? I believe it was consecration. You remember that at one time Barnabas was rather a wealthy man, he had considerable property; but he sold it all and brought the money to the Lord. And as Barnabas gave up that lovely little farm and consecrated everything to the Lord he became marked with the fullness of the Holy Spirit. There was one hymn they used to sing, and it seemed to me they sang it so often—

"I'll go where you want me to go, dear Lord,
Over mountain, or plain, or sea."

I hated that song. I could not sing it, and to hear others do so filled me with dislike. But I well remember that marvelous moment when at last I sat at the foot of the cross and sang from the bottom of my bursting heart, "I surrender all." The next time they sang "I'll go where you want me to go" I quite enjoyed it. The Lord has surely taken me at my word for I have gone all over the world. But oh the joy of consecration!

I find consecration has to be a continuous thing. Since that golden hour many years ago God has enlarged me, I am twice as rich as I was then. My Christian experiences have been piling up, gifts have been piling up; and each time the Lord gives me a little more I have to have a renewed consecration. Would to God everybody would reconsecrate, and that all believers would do that with their spiritual gifts. I remember how almost scared I was when the Lord gave me the gift of tongues. At once I searched and scoured my Bible for all the teaching I could find on how to use the gift of tongues, and I laid it on the altar. Then as the Lord gave me other gifts I laid them on the altar too. I find that consecration is one of the greatest ways for keeping filled with the Spirit.

Perhaps this is what is blocking some of you—there may be something you are not putting on the altar. And although you had the Baptism of the Spirit in the years gone by, you are not filled now with the Spirit, you are not overflowing, you are not in victory, you have not a submissive broken spirit. If once again you lay everything on the altar, I am sure the fire will fall again. Make a fresh consecration before you lay your head on the pillow, and you will be singing in the Spirit tonight.

5

HOLINESS AND SPIRITUAL GIFTS

"A Call to Balance"

It is of the utmost importance concerning spiritual gifts that we should clearly grasp their relationship to the vital subject of holiness. If we fail to do this we shall flounder in ceaseless difficulties and will probably make some bad mistakes in judgment both regarding other people and ourselves.

Several questions press for an answer: questions that are not merely theoretical, but questions that force themselves upon us, sometimes rather jaggedly, from the realm of practical experience. Do spiritual gifts help towards holiness? Do they, or do they not, demand holiness before they can be bestowed? Are they an evidence of holiness? Does the personal holiness of the individual affect their exercise? Are the gifts worth troubling about since holiness is of such supreme importance?

To avoid misunderstanding, we had better observe that by "holiness" in this study we mean Christ-likeness in character: that positive result of salvation by which the very life of Christ is being lived out again in and through the life and character of the believer. There are many outward graces that mark such a character, and foremost among them we may certainly place that beautiful list of what Paul calls in Gal. 5:22, 23 "the fruit of the Spirit." The list is as follows: "Love, Joy, Peace, Longsuffering, Gentleness, Goodness, Faith, Meekness, Temperance." All these he attributes to the work of divine grace in the soul; they are not in the natural soil but come from God.

The Difference between "Gifts" and "Fruit"

It is necessary to clearly understand the fundamental difference between these two terms. "Fruit" is a natural outcome, by a process of steady growth, of a principle of life *within*. "Fruit" takes time to develop, and is brought to perfection by the assistance of much from outside, such as sunshine, rain, soil, etc. "Gifts," on the other hand, may be given by the generous action of someone *without*. They are usually complete as given, though their exercise by the recipient can become more perfect by use, as for instance, in the gift of a camera, or an automobile. The essentials for our present study are that "fruit" comes gradually from within: while "gifts" come immediately from without. This definition is a little crude, but it helps to clear the necessary difference between the two.

The fruit of the Spirit will thus be seen

as the manifestation and outcome of the divine life put within the believer at regeneration; perhaps appearing almost instantly in some features, but more generally appearing gradually by a process of "growth in grace." Its development will be helped by such outward means of grace as Christian fellowship and ministry, circumstances,—and above all, communion with God. There is room for such "fruit," to grow throughout the whole course of a Christian's life; and holiness when viewed from this angle should be steadily progressive.

Gifts of the Spirit, on the other hand, can be bestowed suddenly at any point in the believer's experience. The plain inference of the New Testament is that a gift was given to some believers when they first received the Holy Spirit. Other gifts were given at different crises of the Christian pathway (e. g., 1 Tim. 4:14—most likely at Timothy's being set apart for the work of the ministry —Acts 16:1-3). Still further gifts might be desired and prayed for at any time. 1 Cor. 12:31; 14:13, 39. The bestowal of gifts of the Holy Spirit thus appears to be more or less independent of a believer's maturity of growth in grace; except, of course, as the Lord may mark the fitness of the individual. They do not seem to spring from the life within, but are the sovereign acts of the great Giver.

Love Is Not a Spiritual "Gift"

The first and greatest *fruit* of the Spirit is love. So marvelous is this divine love manifested in and through the life wholly yielded to the Spirit of Christ, that when Paul devotes a whole chapter (1 Corinthians 13) to its praises we feel that he is practically describing the ideal Christian.

Let us be quite clear that such love is a "fruit" rather than a "gift." It is distinguished from spiritual gifts in 1 Cor. 14:1. It is quite un-Scriptural to say, "I am seeking love, the greatest gift of all." Many say this, but Love is not mentioned among the nine gifts of the Spirit. 1 Cor. 12:8-11. Instead of expecting the character of 1 Corinthians 13 to be dropped suddenly and completely into the heart as a finished gift from God, we should rather see that it is the fruit of the working out of a divine principle within. It is perfected by a life of close communion with the Lord, and in no other way.

Taking love as described so exquisitely in 1 Corinthians 13 as being not only the first fruit of the Spirit (Gal. 5:22), but as also practically embracing all the other "fruit of the Spirit," we are now in a position to note two significant facts written upon the very surface of the New Testament as to the relationship between the "gifts" and the "fruit," as follows:

(a) That there are *nine gifts* recorded in

1 Cor. 12:8-11, and *nine fruits* recorded in Gal. 5:22, 23.

(b) That the great chapter on Love (1 Cor. 13) is embedded between the two principal chapters dealing with Spiritual Gifts, and is an integral part of the subject.

The first fact teaches us that the gifts and the fruit are meant to balance one another: the second that they are intimately connected with one another.

Paul's exhortation concerning "a more excellent way" in the last verse of 1 Corinthians 12 is often interpreted as though he had written: "Don't trouble about spiritual gifts, only seek love." This is quite wrong; he does not write: "Follow after love *instead of* spiritual gifts"; but "Follow after love *and desire* spiritual gifts." It is quite unbalanced and un-Scriptural to ignore or neglect spiritual gifts as so many do.

A Call to Balance

When the apostle writes, "Covet earnestly the best gifts, and yet shew I unto you a more excellent way," he is *not* suggesting that we neglect spiritual gifts. He is giving a call to *balance,* and a correction of spiritual values. The greatest thing of all is increasing likeness to Christ, and it is a huge mistake to think that "gifts" can take the place of "fruit."

He enlarges on this in the opening verses of 1 Cor. 13 with tremendous force. He represents spiritual gifts as operating in their most brilliant capacities—and then brings the whole picture to nought with a crash! The gifts of tongues, of prophecy, of the word of knowledge, and of faith—all equally come beneath his castigating rod. The whole argument centers round those who exercised these gifts and had not love. It is an arresting passage. It must admittedly be a passage of tremendous importance to all who claim a Pentecostal experience.

Note carefully that he does not for one moment question the genuineness of the gifts displayed (as so many hastily do today) and suggest that they were "counterfeits" and came from some demon power. They were genuine gifts of the Holy Ghost, received in the first instance directly from the Lord Himself, but now being exercised by believers who had lost their sense of true spiritual values. Some may be puzzled because their only conception of spiritual gifts is that they represent nothing but a pure working of the Holy Spirit. The whole teaching of these chapters, however, is that the use of spiritual gifts, once bestowed, is open to the will of the individual. 1 Cor. 14:14, 19, 28, 32. The ideal position is where there is such a conformity of the will of the believer to the will of God that all exercise of the gifts is truly "in the Spirit." This is not always so; but it should be the aim of all who exercise spiritual gifts.

What is the result of exercising gifts without love? It is a *two-fold failure:* (a) The exercise is powerless and irritating towards others; (b) the one who exercises the gift receives no benefit himself. (Note the word "nothing" in verses 1-3.) Putting it in plain language, it amounts to this: (a) A Christian who exercises spiritual gifts without a life behind it that corresponds does not make a scrap of impression for good on other people, and is only a continual source of stumbling; (b) A Christian who thinks that by the abundant exercise of spiritual gifts he can make up for lack of personal holiness is miserably deceived.

Therefore he proceeds to detailed teaching on the principles that should govern their exercise, and *love* is the key. Chapter 14 is the practical application of chapter 13 to the proper use of spiritual gifts. Love will not be satisfied by a purely selfish enjoyment of any gift (verse 4, etc.) Love will have a vehement desire to see others blessed (verse 19, etc.) Love will be specially careful not to cast a stumbling-block before anyone (verse 26, etc.) All this brings us back to the perfect balance between the gifts and the fruit. The Christian who has most of the fruit of the Spirit will be the Christian who will most profitably exercise the gifts of the Spirit. A spectacular display of gifts, however dazzling, will produce nothing of eternal value. It needs the vessel to be controlled by the love of God. The character of the believer exercising a spiritual gift may not affect very much its outward manifestation, but it will have a big effect upon its power for solid edification. This is of vital importance.

It is as impossible as it is un-Scriptural to conceive of any revival continuing in the power of the Holy Spirit which only welcomes Him as the inspirer of word or deed, and not of personal holiness also. To *"grieve"* the Spirit of God by lack of sanctification (Eph. 4:30) must inevitably end in *"quenching"* the Spirit of God in His manifestation also. 1 Thess. 5:19. The divinely balanced plan revealed in the New Testament is where the Holy Spirit is alike the source both of fruit and of gift; and for both blessed phases of our redemption He is welcome and obeyed.

Spiritual Gifts in Unsanctified Believers

This presents such a problem to some people that it must be dealt with thoroughly.

The New Testament presents no problem in the matter at all. The confusion arises through some mistaken, and we fear very un-Scriptural, ideas which have been taught.

There is first of all the error that receiving the Baptism of the Spirit makes a child of God sinlessly perfect, or something approaching thereto. The Scriptural truth is that following the Baptism of the Spirit there may be a great amount of personal sanctification still needed in the believer, and this will proceed as the child of God now goes on to "*walk* in the Spirit." Gal. 3:2, 3 and 5:16-25. It is vain to think that any "crisis" or "blessing" or "experience" can take the place of a continual "walking" in the Spirit—however helpful such a crisis may often undoubtedly be.

It is impossible to go into the large question of Scriptural Holiness here; but we may point out that the New Testament names *three* divine agencies for the sanctification of the believer: The Blood (Heb. 8:12), The Word (John 17:17), and The Spirit (1 Peter 1:2). The Baptism in the Holy Spirit is granted upon repentance and remission of sins; the prerequisite condition of a clean heart being received by faith in the precious Blood. Acts 2:38; 15:9. The purpose of the Baptism is power to witness (Acts 1:8) in the various ways granted by the Spirit.

Love Eternal—Gifts Transient

Love is eternal. Its full growth, its finest flowers, never bloom in this land of dim vision and imperfect understanding. They will only appear yonder.

Therefore the soul that is increasing in love is already growing for eternity. To rightly appreciate love is to evidence a true sense of values that has been already adjusted to the everlasting Standard.

Viewed from this high and ultimate standpoint, spiritual gifts assume their true perspective. Even the best gifts shall one day "vanish away." In contrast with that which is eternal they are but transient after all.

Yet even this truth needs safeguarding. The contrast between love and spiritual gifts must be carefully defined. The gifts are transient, they are to "fail," to "cease," to "vanish away." *But not until* "that which is perfect is come" (verse 10). The Greek word for "perfect," *teleois,* means "ended or complete." The vision of the apostle runs right on into the future. The coming of the "perfect" is not in *time* at all, it is in *eternity*: it is not "now," but "then." Until that glorious consummation is arrived at, the gifts of the Spirit will continue.

Moreover, the passage gives no justification for distinguishing (as some have sought to do) between any particular gifts, and so work up an artificial inference that certain gifts will "cease" before others. They are treated as a whole; and the Scripture gives no indication that "tongues" will cease any sooner than "knowledge" will vanish away.

So long as ministry is needed on earth, spiritual gifts will be needed also. For it is the divine gift that makes the ministry and "sets" it in the church (chap. 12:28). The parallel passage in Eph. 4:11-16 may well supply us with the concluding illustration of the true relationship between holiness and spiritual gifts. Here these gifts may be regarded as part of the divinely appointed scaffolding erected on purpose for the "building up" (edifying) of the body of Christ, "till we all come . . . unto a *perfect* man, unto the measure of the stature of the fullness of Christ." They are only needed "till" (note the time limit).

It is obvious that the "scaffolding" will be done away when the building is complete and eternal love is manifested for ever in the glorified church. But until that time it is the height of folly and presumption to endeavor to dispense with any part of the scaffolding. It may well be that parts of that scaffolding which we deem least necessary, are the very parts most needed for the divine Spirit's finishing touches. Let us retain it all; let us jealously guard *every* gift of the Spirit.

He is mistaken indeed who makes more of the scaffolding than the building: but he is scarcely less mistaken who would dispense with the scaffolding before the building is completed. So, likewise, he is greatly mistaken who thinks that the possession of spiritual gifts is of more importance than increase in love and all that makes for Christian character. But he is likewise mistaken who thinks he can do without the gifts, and yet become perfect in holiness according to the mind of God.

"Follow after love—and desire spiritual gifts."

6

HOW TO DISCERN THE VOICE OF THE SPIRIT

Given at Eureka Springs Camp Meeting

"Now there were in the church that was at Antioch certain prophets and teachers. . . . As they ministered to the Lord, and fasted, the Holy Ghost said, Separate me Barnabas and Saul for the work whereunto I have called them. And when they had fasted and prayed, and laid their hands on them, they sent them away. So, they, being sent forth by the Holy Ghost, departed." Acts 13:1-4.

Here the whole church receives the direct voice and leading of the Holy Spirit. As the assembly at Antioch ministered to the Lord, and fasted, the Holy Ghost said something. It does not say how He spoke; and after all, the method by which He speaks is a very secondary matter. The first verse tells us there were prophets and teachers there, and I should imagine that the probability is that the Holy Spirit spoke through the prophets; however it might not have been that way. Notwithstanding all the rubbish and confusion that has come through so-called prophets bringing forth things from their own minds, I do thank God there is a real and true prophecy; and I am quite prepared to believe that the

Holy Ghost will still speak to us through prophets and prophesyings.

Sometimes He speaks through visions. I believe there are visions which are caused by what we ate for supper; but on the other hand God still guides by visions, and some of our visions and dreams can really be inspired by the Holy Spirit.

Friends of mine in whom I have the highest confidence, have told me they have heard the audible voice of God speaking. I believe that is possible. We can still hear the very audible voice of God.

The Spirit of God speaks by that wonderful inward witness also. I love that—that quiet voice which speaks in your heart like the bells of evening. Sometimes it says "yes" and sometimes it says "no"; sometimes it says "amen," and sometimes it gives a word of warning.

Over on the other side of the Atlantic we are bothered with a "church" which is guided very largely by so-called "prophets," and everybody is put into office by the "prophet." He will rise and say, "Yea behold verily My people, thus saith the Lord, John is to be a prophet. Yea behold verily My people, thus saith the Lord, Bill Smith is to be a teacher." And these are put into office regardless of whether or not they have a gift fitting for that office. But the way God puts a man in office is by giving him a gift for the task.

Years ago a friend of mine had a desire to

be a preacher. (It is a strange thing how people who cannot preach want to be preachers.) One day some of these folks who believe in doing everything through a prophet came to his church to set it in order. In the little church there were seven men and a sprinkling of women and children. The prophet got busy. "Yea behold verily my people, thus saith the Lord," until six of these men were put in office. Oh how the prophet prophesied over my friend! "Yea behold verily My people, thus saith the Lord, thou shalt preach, and multitudes shall be turned to the way of righteousness," and so on. My friend wrote me such an enthusiastic letter. He said, "Donald, I cannot tell you how happy I am; I am going to be a preacher. You know how I have always wanted to be one, and you know I have no gifts that way; but the prophet has said I am going to be one and I am so happy."

Time went on, seven, eight, nine months, and still my friend was not preaching. He began to get a little puzzled. After eighteen months I received another letter from him, and oh what a letter it was! Oh the bitterness, the disillusionment when he realized that he had been the victim of an unscriptural error and a foolish fraud. And that is where the danger lies in this false prophesying. While the prophesying is going on, people are swept off their feet, but the danger comes when the disillusionment has arrived. My friend was so bitter that for six months he hovered in the balance and was strongly tempted to backslide into the world. And only God knows the praying some of us had to do for him. But God held him steady and today he is an elder in the church and is doing a most useful work.

My friends, when God calls you to a work He gives you a gift for it. If you have not the gift, then God has not called you to that task. It is the gift that makes the ministry. Don't be in such a hurry to put labels on yourselves, wait till you have the sample, and then put the label on afterwards. Some men go around calling themselves "pastors." They tell you they want their mail addressed to "Pastor So-and-So." Before a man has any right to be called a pastor it should be manifest that God has given him a pastor's heart and ministry. I know of men who split up churches and yet call themselves pastors. Some call themselves an evangelist but they are not that and could not be if they tried. One time I went to a meeting and found myself advertised (I detest publicity) in big letters outside, *"Donald Gee, the Great Scottish Evangelist."* I stood up in the first meeting and said, "I shall have to correct a misunderstanding. In the first place I am not great, in the second place I am not Scottish, and in the third place I am not an evangelist." I am not an "evangelist"; the Lord has made me something else. The gift and the ministry God has given us indicate the office.

The people who set churches in order through the prophets, quote this passage, "Separate me Paul and Barnabas." But notice that the call was not to office, it was to a definite bit of ministry. He called them to what we call the first missionary tour. And the work He called them to was definitely finished, as we see in Acts 14:26; "And thence sailed to Antioch, from whence they had been recommended to the grace of God *for the work which they had fulfilled.*" As far as the personal call to office was concerned it had come to those men long before; Paul had had those three wonderful days when he was without sight, before Ananias came to him in Damascus. The call to work and the call to office is the Lord's personal business. Thank God for human ordination, but there is something deeper,—"Mine the blessed ordination of the pierced hand." The real call to work is a personal call from the great Head of the church Himself, coming to you privately, but often confirmed afterwards in the assembly.

Paul and Barnabas went forth with the blessed knowledge that the Holy Ghost had sent them forth. When things are going hard in the work of the Lord, the only thing that keeps us going is the consciousness that we are in the will of God. There come times for us all when men frown, when we encounter unpopularity, when we are friendless and alone, when the pulling is hard, when the Lord lets us know not only how to abound but how to suffer want. When times like that come, thank God we know we are doing the task because God sent us to it. I don't believe the missionaries could go through what they do, if it were not for the consciousness that God has called them. Many a pastor would not stay in his church another week if he did not know in his heart that God had called him there.

So these two men go forth knowing the Holy Ghost has sent them. And the first place they go, a gifted man stands up and opposes them. But with the confidence that God has called them and that therefore the anointing is upon them, they rebuke him in the name of the Lord and blindness comes upon him. They go on to another place and stones are thrown at them. Some people have an idea that you are not in God's will unless everything is going easily. After the stoning experience they had one still more trying, for the people of the next place think they are gods and bring out garlands to place around them. Lots of our Pentecostal preachers were close to the Lord while they were getting stones, but now that flowers are coming their way——? It is not often men will thunder at those who are throwing flowers at them, and tell them to clear that rubbish away. But these men came off more than conquerors, except one of them—young John Mark.

Possibly you have wondered why Paul took such a serious view of Mark's going back to Jerusalem—running home to his mother. Later on when Barnabas wanted to take Mark with them again, Paul said, "No, we won't have him." The contention grew so sharp between them they parted asunder. Why did Paul take such a serious view of Mark's declension? Because the Holy Ghost had sent them forth, and Mark knew it; and his turning back from the path the Spirit had led them on was a serious business. However, the Spirit had not said, "Separate me Barnabas and Saul *and Mark.*"

(a) Notice the atmosphere in which the Holy Ghost spoke. It is the only atmosphere in which He can guide us. "As they ministered to the Lord, and fasted, the Holy Ghost spake." Oh I wish we had more of that! I wonder how many times we really come to meeting to minister *to the Lord.* I believe most times we come to minister to one another, or to sing to one another. *I would that more of our hymns were hymns of worship.* Seventy-five per cent of our singing today is about ourselves, about our feelings and experiences. It is time we came to church to sing about the Lord. It would be a good thing to set aside one or two meetings where we came to minister to the Lord, came to bring *Him* something. He gives us many good times; would not it be lovely to say, "Lord Jesus, I want to give You a good time, to worship and praise You, telling You how much I love You."

As they waited upon God the feverish activity of their own will and desires dropped off, and they came into a place of quietness where God could speak. Many times we cannot hear the voice of God because we are not quiet enough. These people ministered to the Lord and fasted, and as they waited they came into the place where their own desires, plans and ambitions dropped off. To get into the place where you can really sort out that which is your own mind and that which is the mind of God, takes time. You cannot get to the place where you discern between the two by dropping on your knees and saying breathlessly, "O Lord, guide me!" The trouble with our "leadings from the Lord" has been that we have mixed so much of our own desires in, and have not waited before God long enough to get rid of our own plans and ambitions.

I am talking about things that wreck lives. I know men and women now in middle life, and growing toward old age, whose lives have been wasted because of failure to observe the principle I am trying to teach now. If you want to know the will of God, take time to know it. Be prepared to pray all night if need be. To wait on God until He can sift you out and you can get to know the difference between that which you want and that which God wants. My friend, wait until you hear the moving in the top of the mulberry trees, until you have let God sift out that which you want.

Some people go to the mission field simply with the idea of living a romantic life. But when they get there they won't think there is much romance in it. I was interesting my boy David with a magnetic compass and I showed him how the needle always pointed to the north. Then I played a joke on him. I had a magnet in my pocket and I slipped my hand in and drew it out, very carefully concealing it. Then I began to draw my hand over the compass and make the little needle go here, there and everywhere. David said, "What has gone wrong with it, why it is pointing south!" I said, "If you wait a minute perhaps we can make it point east." That is what some people do with the guidance they receive of the Holy Spirit. They make the compass point anywhere they want it to go, because they have a magnet in their hand. Not long ago a lady came to a friend of mine and said, "Mr. So-and-So, the Lord has told me that I am to marry you." Fortunately the Lord gave him the word of wisdom and he answered, "Well sister, we had better wait until the Lord tells me too." When you examine that lady's leading you can almost see the magnet sticking out of her handbag. Before you become so sure the Lord is leading you a certain way I would advise you to empty your spiritual pockets to see whether you have a few magnets lying there.

(b) Another important principle in the story is that when the Holy Spirit spoke in that assembly, the voice of the Spirit was *collectively* heard and understood, and was *collectively* agreed to and obeyed. Make a note of that. Some people think they are the ones God speaks to, and the rest are so backslidden that they cannot hear His voice. If you could read their minds you would see something like this, "As to the General Council, pooh! it is far too carnal to ever know the mind of the Lord! And as to the Executive Presbytery, it is all carnal!" There are some people who are so individualistic, so loose and rebellious, that they cannot submit to their brethren for five minutes. Those folk always make a mess of things, and they always will; they may succeed for awhile, but they will some time crash, for God has no room for individualists. The church of Christ is a *body* and we are members one of another.

Oh the young men all over the world who won't submit to the elders, who insist on going here and everywhere, freelances! My dear young brethren, this is not God's plan. If the Holy Ghost has spoken to you (and I am not suggesting He has not), He has also spoken to us. And I believe with all my heart that if the Lord has called you, the godly elders of the flock will have a witness to it. I refuse your impudent assertions that we are backslidden. I don't apologize for saying this. I want to say to you young men who think God has called you and has not told us about it, that you are impudent. The Word of God respects elders, and God respects elders. My dear friends, we need one another. I am thankful from the bottom of my heart that I am not traveling around the world as a freelance. We are members of a body. Before I left the Old Country I got the brethren to give me a certificate that I was leaving Great Britain by the consent and with the prayers and agreement of the Presbytery. And when I went to Canada I put myself in the hands of the Canadian Council. I said, "Here I am, brethren, I will go where you want me to go." And it is my happy privilege to work in co-operation with the brethren here.

If I were you, and had what I felt was a revelation from the Lord, I would want to submit it to my brethren. Notice what the apostle says about prophets and prophesyings, "Let the prophets speak two or three, and *let the others judge.*" 1 Cor. 14:29. If there is anything questionable in their prophesyings he does not say to stop them at it, to quench it. That is what some pastors have very foolishly done, and they have driven the prophet away from the assembly and she has started prophesying in Mrs.

Brown's kitchen, and then they have had no end of a job on hand. If anybody in my assembly had a questionable gift I would encourage them to exercise it in public; then I could deal with it. Gifts are not put in Mrs. Brown's kitchen, they are put in the church. If any of you are rebels by exercising your gifts in little private meetings I want to say bring them back into the camp. The *church* is the place for gifts. There it can be checked up. Don't you like being checked up? The Lord help us to see the need of one another. If the prophet refuses to let the others judge his gift, he always becomes a fanatic. The safety of prophecy *in the church* is that we can check one another up.

But if this is true of prophets it is every bit as true of teachers. As soon as a teacher becomes unteachable he is finished. As soon as he becomes dogmatic and bigoted, his usefulness is gone. I am thinking of one of our most precious and beautiful teachers who used to be such a blessing, but for the last few years that man's ministry has been dried up, he is not wanted anywhere. What has gone wrong? He has lost the capacity of being teachable himself. He has become dogmatic and bigoted. My esteemed brethren, fellow ministers and teachers, if you ever hear me utter a word of doctrine which you question, I want to ask you to do me the kindness of coming to me and telling me, because you will be my greatest friend. It may be that in a moment of unrecognized pride we shall think we have a revelation from the Lord when we have not. The whole body is completed by that which every joint supplieth. And so when the Holy Spirit speaks I thank God there are lots of people to check it up. There are some people who say the Lord has spoken to them, and if you don't see it that way it is because you are a back number. You have all heard of the mother who was watching the recruits go by, and she exclaimed, "What a pity, they are all out of step but my boy!" There are lots of saints like that, they think we are all out of step but them. Don't you deceive your little soul, probably it is just the other way around. There are some teachers who feel we are all wrong but them. *The Holy Ghost dwells in the body, and the body is the best safeguard.*

(c) I finish with the deepest note of all; and God help me to speak with a hushed spirit. When the Holy Ghost separated Paul and Barnabas for that work He was leading in a pathway of sacrifice, and I believe He always leads us in the way of sacrifice, in the way of the cross. But I always feel safest of all when I am treading in a path that has an element of suffering in it, because I believe it is the path God's children must travel until they reach the goal. The Holy Ghost said, "Give me Paul and Barnabas, two of your best workers," and the church might have replied, "We cannot spare them, they are our very best." Eight years ago the Lord gave to my church in Edinburgh a young woman worth her weight in gold, she was a gem. Then the Lord came to the assembly and said, "Give me her, I want her for a missionary in China." Did not I rebel! I said, "Lord, we cannot spare her." But thank God we did say, Yes, and today she is in China.

And then there was a sacrifice on the part of Barnabas and Paul. For if the assembly loved them, they loved the assembly; why, Barnabas was its father! And I guess he had a bit of real tussling before he was willing. Pentecostal ministers must remember sacrifice. Directly our ministry loses the sacrifice element we have lost our power. God keep us where we are still a suffering people. If there is anything I tremble about it is about money coming to this movement. I want lots more money to come in, but I want it to go out as quickly as it comes in. God save us from ever having pastorates with big bloated salaries. Some of our precious brethren over in Europe are nearly starving and cannot keep their wives and children. But that is where revival is. God keep us with a suffering ministry, one that is dipped in blood. "Death worketh in us," says the apostle, "but life in you." And the more we give ourselves to death, the more we will minister life to the people. "The good Shepherd giveth His life for the sheep."

7

BAPTIZED TO BE AN "INTERPRETER"

In Job 33:23 there is a word which represents the longing of my own heart, and I believe it represents the longing of many hearts—"An Interpreter." I have a great longing to be an interpreter. I am not referring to the gift of interpretation of tongues; but in the biggest, broadest sense of the word I long to be an interpreter between God and the human soul.

What is an interpreter? It is one who makes things plain and clear. Perhaps someone has a message for you, but he speaks a language you cannot understand; then if there be an interpreter he can cause you to understand, for he can put it in your own language. To be an interpreter it is necessary that you know both languages perfectly. If you are going to interpret a Swedish message to an American, you must understand both the Swedish and the English languages, and you must know them well. And if we are going to be interpreters between God and men we have to know both languages.

I believe the weakness usually is that we don't understand God's language well enough. We don't live in close enough fellowship with God; we don't spend enough time in the heavenly courts, and don't know the language of heaven.

But there is another class of people whose weakness is just the opposite of that, and to them I want to say, "It is time you got back to earth again." Do you know it is possible to live such an other-worldly life (please don't misunderstand me), to get into an unearthly, abnormal spiritual condition, where you may be *very* spiritual but you are not a scrap of good as an interpreter because you have gotten out of touch with men. The Lord Jesus lived a man among men, and I want to do the same. It is possible to have a sticky, sickly spirituality which is unearthly. The Lord keep us normal and healthy, sane and balanced! If you are going to win men you must be manly. The Baptism of the Holy Ghost does not make us unnatural. It should make us beautifully and sweetly normal.

I was attending a street meeting one time and listening to a fine young woman giving her testimony. She was full of the Holy Ghost, on fire for God, and had a real desire to win souls. She was talking to a bunch of coal miners and drunkards, and saying to them, "Dear ones," this. . . . "Dear ones," that. . . . "Dear ones," etc. They were not dear ones by a long way, and they did not like being called dear ones! You see she had lived in the sugary sweet atmosphere of Pentecostal prayer meetings and had lost contact with the world. Prayer meetings are fine, God help us to attend more of them, but we must also keep our contact with mankind. If we live in an atmosphere of camp meetings, and shut ourselves in a glass house, and want to get sent to heaven labelled "Wrapped up with care," we lose that human touch which appeals to men and women, and we cease to be interpreters between God and man. I am speaking this way because I have seen so much of this.

I *do* want to see Pentecostal people kept healthy and normal. I do want to see them the sort of men and women that appeal to other men and women, so that they may be interpreters. If we are going to be interpreters between God and man we have to understand both languages.

But with most of us the difficulty is the other way. When it comes to interpreters, those who understand the things of God and can make them understandable to men are very rare. There are many preachers but not many interpreters. The Book says, "If there be one among a thousand." That is not a very good proportion. A brother said to me today, "You know there are very few really good preachers." He did not mean that they had not a flow of language, that they had not good words and thoughts, but he meant there were few *interpreters*. I find that the man who has a message from God can get the crowd. There are one or two men in Edinburgh who have such a crowd in their church on Sunday night that you have to go early to get a seat. The reason is they are able to make the things of God and eternity and time real to men.

The need of interpreters is spoken of in Job 33:14, "For God speaketh once, yea twice, yet man perceiveth it not." God speaks, but man does not perceive or understand His voice. I absolutely repudiate the suggestion that God is not speaking today. I believe He is speaking as loudly as ever, but men perceive it not. God has spoken in every age. Don't talk to me about the silence of God. I don't believe there is such a thing. God is speaking, but man perceives it not, because there is such a dearth of interpreters.

There are two or three ways of God's speaking and man's not perceiving. One is in Job 33:15, "In a dream, in a vision of the night, when deep sleep falleth upon man, in slumberings upon the bed." Oh, the need of interpreters when God speaks in supernatural ways! This Pentecostal movement, which has come from God to restore the supernatural in His church, is not understood; it is misjudged. In the days of our Lord's flesh when God spoke from heaven, what did they say? Some said it thundered. There is a loose idea among us that if only God did enough supernatural things men would be bound to hear. Scripture does not confirm that idea. Run rapidly through your Bible and note that when angels first appear to men, and man makes his first contact with the supernatural, his first emotion is always fear. You will find the first word the angel usually says, is "Fear not!" Even in Bethlehem's plain when the angelic host came with the sweetest message man ever heard, their first message had to be, "Fear not." If an angel came here this afternoon most of you would run for your lives. When God speaks in supernatural ways there needs to be an interpreter. Miracles do not convert people; they only draw people's attention; and when the attention is drawn there needs to be an interpreter of the word and mind of God.

Sometimes God seeks to stir up an uneasy conscience by dreams and visions in the night. Then how much an interpreter is needed! God does it that He may "keep back their soul from the pit, and their life from perishing by the sword." But folk get the idea that God is going to punish them; they do not understand His loving father-heart. Their conscience may be lashing them until life is unbearable, still God is love, but they need an interpreter to make them see it.

While motoring along in Algiers, North Africa, visiting mission stations, I noticed all along the side of the road big poles carrying high tension electric wires. On the poles were notices, printed in the French language, warning men not to climb the poles and touch the wires lest they be instantly killed. But the natives of Algiers cannot understand the French language, so the French Government had skull and cross-bones painted on each pole—they could understand that language. It was not the purpose of the government to terrify the natives by those skull and cross-bone signs; it was to save them from death. And sometimes God has to scare folks in some way. It is not because He wants to frighten us; He wants to save us. Oh, that He had more interpreters!

I want to show you something else that needs interpreting, and to God's children themselves. Job 33:19, "He is chastened also with pain upon his bed, and the multitude of his bones with strong pain; so that his life abhorreth bread, and his soul dainty meat. His flesh is consumed away, that it cannot be seen; and his bones that were not seen stick out. If there be an interpreter. . . . " I am old fashioned enough to believe that God still speaks to men through sickness. I am not going back an inch on divine healing, but I believe the Lord sometimes has to let the devil touch our bodies because it is the only way He can get our ears. Sickness and disease are still ways by which He speaks when He cannot get our ears any other way. The folks in the early Corinthian church were falling sick, and some of them dying, and they could not make out why it was. But an "interpreter" came along. He said, "*For this cause* many are weak and sickly among you, and many sleep." For what cause? Eating and drinking unworthily, and not discerning the Lord's body. Thank God for interpreters! If God is having to deal with me in discipline, and I cannot understand, God send me a true friend who will show me the cause.

You know that lovely passage in the epistles where some of them are puzzled because they have been chastened and trouble has come. Thank God there was an interpreter who could tell them that "whom the Lord *loveth* He chasteneth." Some preachers tell you that when you are saved you will have no troubles; and if only you get the Baptism of the Spirit it will be glory all the way. I find it isn't that way. The first thing that happened to my Lord after He was baptized was that the Spirit drove Him into the wilderness to be tempted of the devil. I sometimes feel I want to put my arms around God's Pentecostal people. Some leaders have the idea that when folks receive the Baptism they are fixed, but lots of times they need help more then than ever before. My heart goes out to those baptized in the Spirit who are left to flounder, with the idea that now they have the Baptism they know everything. Bless their hearts, they are only beginning! Pentecostal people need a tremendous amount of help. That is why I am practical, and am talking "brass tacks" to you. We need interpreters even in our Pentecostal experience.

My dear suffering friend, I want to cheer your heart. God is letting you be in that school of suffering because He wants you to learn certain lessons. When they are learned, then He will give you the joy of being an interpreter to other suffering ones, to tell them that God draws us nearer to Himself in the thick cloud and in the darkness. I find there is a need of learning all I can in every experience of life if I am to be a help to others. I thank God I am a married man with a family. When I go around to pay pastoral calls and they tell me about Tommy and Nellie and Mary having the whooping-cough and measles, I can understand why those little things came to my own family—it enables me to understand. Then I tell the people how we pray for the children and the Lord heals. I am glad to have the experiences of life. My brother, thank God for your circumstances. Don't complain and complain and grumble, for God is training you to be an interpreter. Learn the secret of the situation you are in, learn the message and purpose of it. And thank God you can be able to help multitudes of others.

I finish on the highest note of all. I finish, "looking unto Jesus the Author and Finisher of our faith." He was and is and ever will be the Greatest Interpreter of all. God was in heaven; man had lost contact with Him, was dead in trespasses and sin, and had ceased to understand God. But there was One who came out of the ivory palaces, from the heart of the Father, down from the glory, and He became a very man among men. He came down to the village of Nazareth, to the carpenter's shop, to be one in a big family. He had not the same father as the rest of them, but He had all the family life just the same. And when James or Joses struck his finger with a hammer, Jesus had to comfort him. And when some of them quarreled, Jesus had to straighten things out. But because of that, He became an interpreter. "There is one God, and one Mediator between God and men, the man Christ Jesus." In those matchless parables of His He was really interpreting God. In the parable of the prodigal son He was not teaching about prodigals. We know about them without being told, but He was interpreting the heart of the Father and making people see that God was waiting and longing to have those prodigals come back.

The Lord help us to interpret the Father. I believe it is for this purpose that God has baptized us in the Holy Ghost, not to take us out of the world, but to give us *power* to live *in* the world as interpreters, interpreting the love of the Redeemer to the souls He died to save.

8

THE FRUIT OF THE SPIRIT

"Temperance" *(Self-Control)*

There are still many people to whom "temperance" is specially connected with strong drink; but it is almost unnecessary to point out that true temperance has a wide application to every one of our appetites, not only all the bodily ones, but all the mental and spiritual ones, too. "Temperate in *all things*" is the aim of Paul. 1 Cor. 9:25. It is possible to be abstemious to the point of "neglecting the body" (Col. 2:23), and yet be hopelessly immoderate in temper, or in the use of the tongue, or in love of praise or power.

Samson was a Nazarite from his birth (Judges 16:17), which signified total abstinence from wine and strong drink; yet he is one of the saddest examples on record of a man with practically no self-control where other passions were concerned. "Self-control" is the finest definition of true Scriptural temperance, and is, indeed, the actual translation used in several places in the Revised Version, as Acts 24:25; 2 Peter 1:5; etc. It is this quality of character known as "self-control" which is a fruit of the Spirit.

Self-Control of the Flesh

Lack of self-control of the physical appetites is one of the most prevalent forms of weakness and sin. Paul winged an arrow straight to the mark, that terrified Felix, when "he reasoned of righteousness, *self-control,* and the judgment to come." Acts 24:25, R. V. Some forms of intemperance with the body are not outward and public, like drunkenness, but they are equally deadly to both body and soul. "Abstain from fleshly lusts, which war against the soul." 1 Peter 2:11. Paul's tremendously strong words are worth quoting in full: "Every man that striveth for the mastery is temperate in all things. Now they do it for a corruptible crown; but we an incorruptible. I therefore . . . keep under (buffet) my body, and bring it into subjection." 1 Cor. 9:25-27. Moffatt's translation puts fresh force into some of his words: "Every athlete practices self-restraint all round . . . I maul and master my body." The language used implies constant vigilance, if not constant struggle. The stakes are so high that the soul cannot afford anything less than keeping an absolute mastery over all physical desires. They may serve, but they must never reign. "Let not sin therefore reign in your mortal body, that ye should obey it in the lusts thereof." Rom. 6:12.

The question does not even end with

things commonly called "sinful," which popularly means an outrage on propriety or a breach of moral law. It equally applies to things "lawful," things in which no disobedience to a specific commandment occurs. Indeed, says Paul, "all things are lawful for me, but I will *not be brought under the power* of any." 1 Cor. 6:12. The man or woman who simply *must* have the gratification of this or that fleshly indulgence, and is miserable and thrown out of balance if they cannot enjoy it, is by just that same amount of bondage less free for the service of the Master. We too often limit the application of this principle to champagne or cigarettes; but forget that we can be equally in chains to our cup of coffee, our extra half-hour in bed, our afternoon nap, or our special whims in food. Excellent servants, these things; but miserable masters. "I will not be brought under the power of any" says the free soul. A Christly self-control will use them gratefully when convenient and profitable; but will just as serenely "carry on" when they are not forthcoming.

Self-Control of Our Spirit

There is a striking picture of the lack of this in the Book of Proverbs; "He that hath no rule over his own spirit is like a city that is broken down and without walls" (Ch. 25:28). We can easily imagine that city! Once strong, self-respecting, able to resist all marauders and defend the fruitful gardens all around: now despicable and dejected, no power of resistance to the feeblest attack, overgrown with weeds and rubbish.

For there are passions of the spirit which, ungoverned, can plunge the soul into a wreckage every bit as ruinous as that which comes through unmastered passions of the flesh.

(a) One of the most prevalent is uncontrolled temper. Few who read these lines are likely to be the victims of those outbursts of rage that ultimately bring the soul seemingly, and even actually, under absolute demon-power. But anger can take other forms; it can be morose, gruff, sulky or moody. Yet we seldom hear this called "intemperance"!

(b) An extravagant love of praise and popularity can be another intemperance of the spirit. We all like to be appreciated, and a little bit of it is manna to a hungry soul, and good for us all. But there can grow up within us an inordinate love of the praise of men that holds us in such slavery that we are unwilling to perform any service unless flattered and fawned after, and unable to give a good account of ourselves in that particular line of ministry God has given to us unless coaxed and enthused by crowded and enthusiastically appreciative audiences. If that is so we are in miserable bondage, and severely handicapped in our usefulness.

(c) Another intemperance of the spirit is an unbridled tongue; whether lashing out in passionate anger and cutting sarcasm, or pouring out an unrestrained river of sheer emptiness and gossip. It is possible to become almost intoxicated in some company with the flow of words, words, words. Not long ago the writer was present at a meeting where the anointing of the Spirit had rested so mightily upon the word that a holy awe seemed to rest upon the crowded congregation as it dispersed. Yet it was all dissipated for some by the way they simply let the fullness of their spirits find expression in ceaseless joke and banter in the bus on the way home. There was no self-control. They felt "full-up" after the good meeting, and that seemed the only way they could let it out. It appeared innocent; it was actually tragic.

Or else the mere love of passing on news opens the floodgates until that which ought to have been held in strictest confidence and reserve flows on through the lips—beyond recall. The unhappy regret we feel afterwards is only a part of the price paid for lack of "temperance in all things." The Scriptural word used for mastery of the tongue is "*bridle*" (James. 1:26); and it implies a firm strong *control* of the spirit however enticing the circumstances.

(d) It would be a surprise to many to know that a lack of rule over our own spirits,

—spiritual intemperance—can be the reason for an abuse of spiritual gifts. Paul dealt with this sympathetically, but firmly. He did not forbid speaking with tongues (1 Cor. 14:39); but he insisted upon temperance. Note carefully that his remedy is *self-control*. "Let it be by two, or the most by three, and that by course" (v. 27). "If there be no interpreter, let him keep silence" (v. 28). "The spirits of the prophets are subject to the prophets" (v. 32). Unfortunately many have never learned to distinguish between the moving of their own spirits, by some eloquent and anointed preacher, or some emotional hymn or prayer,—and the true moving of the Holy Spirit upon them to give forth a genuine revelation from the Lord.

An intemperate use of any "sweet" thing always ends in nausea and reaction. The old word of wisdom stands fixedly true—"Hast thou found honey? Eat so much as is sufficient for thee, lest thou be filled therewith and vomit it." Prov. 25:16. A sweet song too often sung, a sweet phrase too often used in preaching or prayer, a sweet spiritual gift too often exercised:—all alike become ultimately tiresome and in danger of being cast away altogether. This often means lasting loss. These things are, like honey, essentially good in themselves if used in moderation. The Scriptural remedy is temperance, not prohibition. To end by being useless to the *Holy Spirit* just because we did not control our own spirits sufficiently, is sad indeed.

Self-Control—Yet Not Self

All this talk about "self-control" savors so much of modernistic teaching rather than sound old evangelical truth that some of our readers will wonder where we are taking them. Yet we cannot have gone far wrong since we have kept to the very words of Scripture. There *is* a place for self-control.

True sanctification, however deeply taught and experienced, will never destroy the personality of the individual, and a genuine Baptism of the Holy Spirit never damages one iota of our power of self-control, or moves our personal responsibility, however mightily filled with God. There is a deep gulf fixed between the Christian led by the Spirit and the spiritist medium carried away by a power they know not of.

The Lord Jesus Christ possessed a radiant personality, perfectly poised, and under complete self-control in every situation. In the judgment hall of Pilate, Christ was probably the only one there who was exercising perfect self-control, though He appeared to be at the mercy of all. He carried His superb balance right to the Cross. The early church faced persecution, sweeping success, overwhelming inner experiences, with the same wonderful poise. If any of the Assemblies showed any signs of losing it there were apostles quickly on hand to restore the equilibruim.

Yet this amazing sanity and self-control, in the face of entirely new spiritual experiences that might have been counted upon to effectually destroy it, existed along with, and indeed because of, an utter and complete surrender of self to One who died for them and rose again. It was so real they said they were "dead"; but they "lived" in Him. Therein lay the open secret: beautifully expressed centuries later by one who wrote, *"My freedom is Thy grand control."*

Self-control as never before is the happy experience of full salvation. And where the poor rags of the last shreds of not only self-control, but self-respect with it, have been torn from the heart that has become the slave of passions of every description, then the message of hope in the Gospel is that in Christ all may be restored. When Jesus comes into the heart, then His Spirit controlling within produces as the final fruit—"temperance in all things."

9

SPIRITUAL GIFTS AND EVANGELISM

Burnt into my memory is an incident that happened several years ago. I had been asked to speak at a small Pentecostal mission in London, but just before the meeting the leader took me aside and gave me the following rather startling words of direction, "We don't go in for spiritual gifts here; we are after souls."

It is only a few weeks since I received a letter from a rather prominent Pentecostal leader in America to the effect that he had observed that the "healthiest" assemblies were generally those that had concentrated on evangelism rather than the gifts of the Spirit.

Here are statements with sufficient implications in them to cause any Pentecostal preacher to do some hard thinking. Why should there be this apparent impossibility of "going in" for spiritual gifts and at the same time pursuing an aggressive evangelism? Why cannot the two be mixed? Where are we out of line with the New Testament?

It is certain that there is no such antagonism in the Scriptures. Those who preached this "great salvation" had their word borne witness to by "gifts of the Holy Ghost." Heb. 2:3-4. A joyful experience of spiritual gifts coupled with a marvelously successful evangelism runs all through the New Testament—from the Day of Pentecost, when speaking with tongues had a sequel in three thousand converts, clear through to Paul's very last epistle in which he bids Timothy to both "stir up the gift of God which is in thee by the putting on of my hands" and also to "do the work of an evangelist." 2 Tim. 1:6; 4:5.

Difficulties in combining an exercise of spiritual gifts with evangelism reveal something wrong with our understanding of either the gifts of the Spirit, or of true evangelism, or of both.

This supposition that the two cannot be combined has become more than an idea; it has become a policy. There are Pentecostal leaders and assemblies who are rightly keen upon aggressive evangelism, and yet feel that the only way they can successfully pursue their object is to frown upon all exercise of spiritual gifts, at least in public meetings. Under such a policy distinctive Pentecostal testimony and experience usually come to a full stop with converts receiving the Baptism with the Holy Spirit. Frequently there gradually creeps in a marked tendency to resort to purely natural methods of attraction to, and conduct of, the services rather than a dependence upon the supernatural power of the Spirit. It is difficult to believe that some of these methods do not actually grieve the Holy Spirit. The vision of a truly New Testament church becomes blurred and lost.

It is only fair to add that there are other leaders and assemblies that make much of at least *some* of the gifts of the Spirit, but are plain failures when it comes to evangelism. Yet they sometimes boast of being "real Pentecost," and regard these others as miserable backsliders. "Real Pentecost" for these folk evidently does not extend beyond the fourth verse of Acts 2; it has no interest in the forty-first verse! Barrenness on the line of soul-winning seems to give them no concern; they are content to stay in their little meetings having "good times," and (presumably) "letting the Lord have His way"; as though the Christ of Calvary had ceased to care any longer for the rolling tide of human woe and suffering. Sometimes these little companies take a commendable interest in foreign missions, but evangelical interest that is centered abroad and not equally as much at home is in danger of becoming merely sentimental, and is certainly not "Pentecostal" in the true Scriptural sense.

Can the Two Be Combined?

Such a question ought never to be seriously asked before an open Bible. They *were* combined in the early church, with conspicuously successful results. They *must* be combined today, if we are to attain to all that "Pentecost" really stands for.

The pre-eminent place of the Holy Spirit in all true evangelism will be conceded by all. It is His particular work to convict of sin, (John 16:8); it is He who lifts up Christ (John 15:26; 16:14); through His gracious energy we are born again. John 3:5. Gifts that come from Him and are His "working" (1 Cor. 12:7-11) cannot, therefore, be antagonistic to evangelism but must have a valuable and well-defined place in all that has to do with soul-winning.

Fortunately we have a wealth of material in the New Testament to demonstrate this. Let us take the gifts of the Spirit one by one.

1. The Word of Wisdom.

Paul decisively puts "words which man's wisdom teacheth" on one side in his planting of Christian churches (1 Cor. 2:13), but he does this only that he may the more conspicuously use those words of wisdom "which the Holy Ghost teacheth." And what is this divine wisdom? It is none other than "Christ crucified." 1 Cor. 1:23-31. In the preaching of Christ and His Cross is contained the very essence of the word of wisdom. And therein lies the heart of the gospel. There can be no clash between *this* spiritual gift and evangelism. An anointed and inspired preaching of "Christ Crucified" is evangelism's foremost weapon. Modern evangelism suffers from exactly that which Paul discarded as unprofitable — "words which man's wisdom teacheth."

That same Spirit-given word of wisdom inspired all his epistles (2 Peter 3:15), and made them such rich soul food for his young converts.

2. Word of Knowledge.

Here we admittedly leave the realm of initial evangelism, for this gift is primarily manifested in doctrine for the building up of the believer. It is those like Apollos who help much those who *have* believed (Acts 18:27) who are most concerned here, the "waterers" who follow the "planter." 1 Cor. 3:6. Yet is is a poor evangelism that makes no provision and manifests no concern for the future growth of the souls it has brought to new birth. Right here is another fundamental weakness with many modern revivals. They are not followed up enough.

Moreover, the word of knowledge (note the "we knows" of the First Epistle of John) forms the one essential basis for evangelism. Unless the evangelist and personal soul-winner have a ringing "we know" about salvation they are only blind leaders of the blind.

3. The Gift of Faith.

The gift of supernatural faith touches the spring of all true spiritual power. It lies at the source of the more openly miraculous gifts that follow; it claims apparently impossible victories over all opposing powers of darkness and defeat; and it finds itself in its own realm in that intercessory prayer and travail for souls which is the hidden source of all true revival and successful evangelism. There will be no need for questionable methods of promoting a revival when and where the spiritual gift of faith has been in operation. Note the success of Stephen. Acts 6:8. Evangelism is helpless without faith.

4. The Gifts of Healing.

It is superfluous to dwell upon the intimate and invaluable connection between the gifts of healing and a Scriptural evangelism. This was first instanced by our Lord Himself, and scarcely less illustriously by those who followed Him. Philip the evangelist had a mighty use for these gifts in his notably successful evangelistic ministry at Samaria. Acts 8. Physical healing often opens the door of the heart to the gospel message as nothing else will do.

5. Working of Miracles.

The same applies to this gift also. Paul's stirring period of brilliantly successful evangelism at Ephesus (Acts 19), was largely connected with God's working "special miracles" by his hands. It should be remembered, however, that mere signs and wonders do not in themselves save any people. Their mission is to attract and arrest, but the preaching of the *Word* saves. The spectacular element in evangelism is always a point of danger, and if that is true of the genuinely spiritual spectacular how much more is it true of cheap sensationalism!

6. The Gift of Prophecy.

The gift of prophecy, or inspired utterance through the Spirit in a known language, is another gift primarily intended for the edifying of believers. 1 Cor. 14:4, 22. It is strikingly stated, however, that when this spiritual gift is being exercised in the church in divine order it has a most powerful and convincing effect upon the unbeliever present (v. 24). Though by no means directly addressed, he may become tremendously convicted. No restrictions are laid down for silencing this gift, even though unbelievers do happen to be present. Obviously it can be used by the Spirit for evangelism of a deeply personal and satisfactory kind. Silas the prophet (Acts 15:32) was a most valuable coworker with Paul in his apostolic evangelism.

7. Discerning of Spirits.

This spiritual gift is one of the safeguards of the church against deception, whether from demon power (as the girl at Philippi, Acts 16); or from hypocrisy (as with Ananias and Sapphira, Acts 5); or from both together (as Simon the sorcerer, Acts 8). The last-named instance is a striking example of the need and value of this gift, even in the midst of remarkably successful evangelistic work. Satan will wreck the most prosperous revival if he can only get in. Sometimes gifted evangelism has suffered severely from lack of discernment in spiritual things.

8. Diversities of Tongues.

This gift is one of God's "signs" to the unbeliever (1 Cor. 14:22), and *must* therefore have a legitimate place on occasions when the unbeliever is present. On the Day of Pentecost it produced a double result of amazement and derision (Acts 2:13, 14), but it plainly had a big part in attracting the attention of the people to the gospel message preached by Peter. The only Scriptural ground, and therefore the only right ground, to take is that this gift is not antagonistic but is positively helpful to evangelism *when rightly used.* If it has proved a hindrance to evangelistic work it can only be because it has been wrongly used, probably by earnest but misguided people.

Perhaps we might add that as a "sign" to unbelievers in connection with evangelistic services we think this gift will be used *by the Holy Spirit* very seldom. "Familiarity breeds contempt," and a "sign" used two or three times in every meeting soon becomes nauseating rather than convicting. Occasionally used, however, it can have startling results, and this would seem to be the divine purpose. We are not referring to private uses of the gift for devotional purposes (1 Cor. 14:2, but to its place in the public meeting.

9. Interpretation of Tongues.

This gift has one unique value in connection with the "unlearned" (which may apparently include the "unbeliever" also (see 1 Cor. 14:23) with whom we are particularly interested in evangelism), in that it brings utterances in "tongues" by the saints in the assembly within the grasp of his understanding. (vv. 13-16). This involves the possibility of the utterance having the same effect upon him as prophesying (v. 24). "Interpretation" is not always necessary when the Spirit is using the gift of tongues for a direct sign to unbelievers. Judging from Acts 2 there are occasions when the tongue spoken will be well enough understood by the one for whom the sign is intended. The gift of interpretation is primarily for the church (v. 5).

Why Are There Difficulties?

Having Scripturally demonstrated that spiritual gifts are not antagonistic to evangelism, but rather an essential part of it, we may well ask the question once again, Why this persistent idea, often developed into a policy, that spiritual gifts and successful evangelism cannot possibly go together.

Let it be freely admitted that in some instances there has been sufficient reason, unhappily, for the stand taken by earnest evangelists for direct discouragement along the line of gifts of the Spirit. We do not blame them. We want to find the way through.

The answer need not imply anything essentially wrong with either the spiritual gifts or the evangelism. It is simply the old, old problem which Paul had to deal with at Corinth in his day. Successful evangelism *there* was in danger of being wrecked by mistakes and abuses with perfectly right gifts. 1 Cor. 14:23. Our troubles and theirs are practically identical, which is also only another indirect proof that "Pentecost" as we know it today is truly from the Spirit of God in spite of its defects. The Corinthian assembly was erring on three lines:

(a) An Unbalanced Valuation of the Gifts (Chap. 12).

They evidently thought that the power of the Spirit was much more manifest in "tongues" than in the word of wisdom or the word of knowledge, where as the reverse was most likely true.

So many precious Pentecostal people today make the same mistake, and scarcely recognize the Spirit's power or gifts except in "tongues." We have even heard leaders refer to utterances in tongues as the Spirit speaking, with a strong inference that He has been silent unless that one particular gift has been in frequent operation. God forbid! We need to recognize the voice of the Spirit in *all* His various gifts, and if this were so there would probably be less of those disturbing interruptions of evangelists and other preachers by merely emotional utterances in tongues which have probably been one of the prime reasons why ardent evangelists have sometimes felt driven to take an unfortunate and un-Scriptural stand against all use of this gift whatsoever in their meetings. "Tongues" is not the only way the Spirit speaks, and it is little short of a crime to interrupt an anointed preacher by a mere bubbling up of our own spirits.

(b) A Lack of Divine Love (Chap. 13).

True love always thinks of others first. This is the prime motive for evangelism. But the Corinthian believers were not caring about the unbeliever in their midst, so long as they could give full rein to an unbridled enjoyment or display of their own spiritual gifts. Consideration for "others" is Paul's watchword (Ch. 14:17-19), with regard both to fellow believers and to the unbelievers.

We should make very few mistakes with spiritual gifts if we were always controlled above all things by a passion for souls—for "others." It is not the working of the Holy Spirit in evangelistic meetings that we need to be afraid of. He will *never* drive one soul away from the gospel, either during the preliminaries, the preaching, or the altar call. It is the working of our own spirit that needs such careful watching. And that watch should be redoubled in evangelistic services, remembering that the salvation of souls is at stake. A mistake at other times may not matter; a mistake then may be fatal. Better err on the side of personal repression if we err at all. The Spirit is not likely to be very grieved if our motive was carefulness not to hinder a soul's coming to Christ. Every part of an evangelistic service is best left to those who have had experience, and have been proved to know the mind of the Spirit.

(c) A Disorderly Use of Gifts (Chap. 14).

It was not the speaking with tongues that made a danger of people saying that the Corinthian assembly had gone mad; it was if *all* spoke with tongues (14:23); that is, all simultaneously, or an excessive number, and without interpretation. It was a disorderly use of a gift which could be tremendously effective if it were used in the right time and in the right way.

Some people do not think that we need to be taught how to use the gifts of the Spirit, but we do. Not that the Holy Spirit Himself will ever make any mistakes, but our own spirit may, and hence the need of the rules laid down in 1 Cor. 14:27-33, so that we may check up ourselves in these matters. The great ideal is where the Spirit of God so perfectly controls every member of the body of Christ that every operation of a gift is just a "working" of the Holy Spirit (Ch. 12:11). Then we may be sure there will be no hindrance to evangelism or sanctification or any other great work the Spirit is engaged in at the moment. But God's children are at various stages of spiritual understanding. Concerning spiritual gifts the Corinthians were anything but "men" (1 Cor. 14:20), and we fear the same could be written of many of God's precious Pentecostal people today. Hence Paul had to lay down rules which would be quite superfluous if we were always in the Spirit.

The final simple summing up of the whole matter is in Chap. 14:40—"Let all things be done decently and in order." No spiritual gift, *exercised in the Spirit,* will ever violate that rule and therefore will never hinder true evangelism.

Rightly understood and rightly used, the gifts of the Spirit are the church's only adequate equipment for fulfilling her great commission of preaching the gospel to every creature.

